HALL OF SHAME

Bluestreak
BOOKS

An imprint of Weldon Owen International

Printed in Turkey

ISBN: 978-1-68188-760-9

First printed in 2021

10 9 8 7 6 5 4 3 2

Thanks to Mariah Bear, Madeleine Calvi, Ian Cannon, Allister Fein, Lizzie Herald, Katie Killebrew, Chrissy Kwasnik, Lauren LePera, Finn Moore, Sean Moore, and Roger Shaw.

HALL OF SHAME

Andy Herald

Bluestreak
BOOKS

CONTENTS

INTRODUCTION

Congratulations! With this book you have armed yourself with the dadliest and most pun-encrusted quips and jests that everyone loves to hate or simply hates to love.

Either way you are now punstoppable and able to entertain and irritate men, women, and children of all ages. Marvelous.

WHAT EXACTLY IS A DAD JOKE?

The classic Dad joke is a short joke with a punchline that is usually a predictable pun or corny play on words, and commonly judged to be endearingly cheesy or cringe-inducingly unfunny. They're often wholesome, but always awfulsome. Example:

SON: Dad, I'm hungry.
DAD: Hi, Hungry. I'm Dad!

Despite the name, Dad jokes are for everyone! Whether you're male or female, young or old, you don't even need to have kids to inflict these goofy groaners on your unsuspecting victi—uh, your chosen joke recipients.

Read this book pretty much the way that you'd read any other book but do it at a 90-degree angle to stay warm. Kidding! Read it however you'd like. Which is probably going to be on the toilet or maybe even on a riding mower in your backyard. You do you.

SOME POINTERS

Launch yourself into the dadosphere with these tips for how to deliver a good(ish) dad joke.

- First off, realize that the goal isn't to tell a "good" joke, but one that's so cheesy bad that it becomes oh-so good.

- Even if people start groaning like a cow delivering triplets before you've even finished, just keep on dad-joking on!

- It's good form to chuckle or guffaw at your own punchlines, especially since you may be the only one laughing and people just want to punch you.

- Signs you're on a roll: groans, sighs, facepalms, eye twitches, and the occassional dry heave.

IT'S YOUR DOODY!

Laughter really is one of the best medicines, so recognize that you're helping with the health and wellness of society. You're improving the world, you hero, you!

Andy H

Andy Herald
HowtobeaDad.com

ANIMALS

I'm practicing for a bug-eating contest and I've got butterflies in my stomach.

What do you call a gorilla wearing headphones?
Anything you'd like; it can't hear you.

My father has the heart of a lion...
and a lifetime ban from the local zoo.

Why are giraffes so slow to apologize?
Because it takes them a long time to swallow their pride.

Why did the octopus beat the shark in a fight?
Because it was well armed.

What do you get when you cross a bee and a sheep?
A baa-humbug.

Why did the bee get married?
Because she found her honey.

What goes zzub-zzub?
A bee flying backwards.

Where do bees go to the bathroom?
The BP station.

Why do bees have sticky hair?
Because they use honey combs!

What do you call a beehive without bees?
An eehive.

What creature is smarter than a talking parrot?
A spelling bee.

What do you call a bear with no teeth?
A gummy bear!

How do you tell the
difference between a
crocodile and
an alligator?
**You will see one later
and one in a while.**

Why do ducks make great detectives?
They always quack the case.

Why did the Clydesdale give
the pony a glass of water?
Because he was a little horse!

What do you call a
pig with three eyes?
A piiig.

Two silk worms had a race.
They ended up in a tie.

Why did the chicken
get a penalty?
For fowl play.

Knock knock.
Who's there?
Owls say.
Owls say who?
Yes, they do.

What do you call a pig that knows karate?
A pork chop!

My wife told me to take the
spider out instead of killing
it... **we had some drinks,
he's a cool guy, wants to be
a web developer.**

Why do fish live in salt water?
Because pepper makes them sneeze!

Why are fish
so smart?
**Because they live
in schools!**

What did the fish
say when it swam
into a wall?
"Damn!"

Why are fish easy to weigh?
Because they have their own scales.

What do you call two
barracuda fish?
A Pairacuda!

DAD: What do you call a
fish with an eye missing?
KID: I don't know.
DAD: **A Fsh.**

FISH

Where do sheep go to get their hair cut?
The baa-baa shop.

What do you get when you
cross a chicken with a skunk?
A fowl smell!

What do you call
two octopuses that
look exactly the
same? **Itenticle.**

Why do
bears
have hairy
coats?
**Fur
protection.**

What do you call a
fly without wings?
A walk.

Did you know crocodiles
could grow up to 15 feet?
But most just have four.

DAD: A kangaroo can jump higher than the Empire State Building.
SON: No way!
DAD: Of course. The Empire State Building can't jump at all.

Which side of the chicken has more feathers?
The outside.

It's only a murder of crows if there's probable caws.

Knock knock.
Who's there?
Kanga.
Kanga who?
Actually, it's kangaROO.

They tried to make a diamond shaped like a duck. **It quacked under the pressure.**

What's the difference between a seal and a sea lion? **An ion!**

What do you call a monkey in a mine field? **A baboooooom!**

What do you call a snake that's 3.14 feet long? **A π-thon.**

What's the difference between a hippo and a zippo? **One is really heavy and the other is a little lighter.**

Why should you never trust a pig with a secret? **Because it's bound to squeal.**

What kind of dinosaur loves to sleep? **A stega-snore-us.**

Why did the lion eat the tightrope walker? **He wanted a well-balanced meal!**

Just read a few facts about frogs. **They were ribbiting.**

Why did the feline fail the lie detector test? **Because he was a lion.**

How do you know if there's an elephant under your bed?
Your head hits the ceiling!

What do you get when you cross an elephant and a rhino?
'Eliphino!

What's the difference between an African elephant and an Indian elephant?
About 5,000 miles.

Why do you never see elephants hiding in trees?
Because they're so good at it.

What's large, gray, and doesn't matter?
An irrelephant.

Just watched a documentary about beavers. **It was the best dam program** I've ever seen.

What does a female snake use for support? **A co-Bra!**

Knock knock.
Who's there?
Rhino.
Rhino who?
Rhino every knock-knock joke there is!

What do you get if you put a duck in a cement mixer? **Quacks in the pavement.**

What do you call an ant that has been banished by her friends? **A socially dissed ant!**

DAD: You know why crabs never give to charity?
KID: Please don't, Dad.
DAD: **Because they're shellfish.**

What do you call an alligator in a vest? **An investigator!**

Why do cows have hooves instead of feet? **Because they lactose.**

What do you call an owl that does magic tricks? **Hoo-dini.**

How many tickles does it take to tickle an octopus? **Ten tickles.**

So, I heard this pun about cows, but it's kinda offensive so I won't say it. I don't want there to be any beef between us.

Guess what happened to the cow that jumped over the barbed wire fence? Udder destruction.

Why do cows wear bells? Because their horns don't work.

Knock knock.
Who's there?
Cows go.
Cows go who?
No, silly. Cows go "moo!"

What kind of magic do cows believe in? MOOdoo!

ART & MUSIC

The other day I was listening to a jingle about superglue. **It's been stuck in my head ever since.**

Knock knock.
Who's there?
A little old lady.
A little old lady who?
Dang! All this time, I had no idea you could yodel.

I used to be addicted to the hokey pokey, **but then I turned myself around.**

What do you call an eagle who can play the piano? **Talonted!**

What kind
of music
do planets
listen to?
Nep-tunes.

Have you ever heard of a music group
called Cellophane?
They mostly wrap.

Why was the picture
sent to prison?
It was framed.

I used to work for an
origami company,
but they folded.

A doctor broke his leg while auditioning
for a play. **Luckily, he still made the cast.**

I've just written a song about a tortilla.
Well, it's more of a rap really.

Why do choirs keep buckets handy?
So they can carry their tune.

In the news, a courtroom artist was arrested today. **I'm not surprised, she always seemed sketchy.**

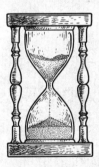

SON: What is this movie about?
DAD: **It's about two hours long.**

What type of music do balloons hate?
Pop music!

I been watching a channel on TV that is strictly just about origami—**of course, it's paper-view.**

How do you make Lady Gaga cry? **Poker face.**

Knock knock.
Who's there?
Keanu.
Keanu who?
Keanu let me in, it's cold out here!

My pet mouse, Elvis, died last night. **He was caught in a trap.**

Why did the opera singer go sailing? **She wanted to hit the high Cs.**

What is the best way to carve wood? **Whittle by whittle.**

Why did Adele cross the road? **To say hello from the other side.**

I just broke my guitar. **It's okay, I won't fret.**

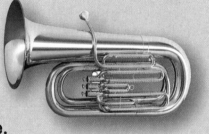

What musical instrument is found in the bathroom? **A tuba toothpaste.**

DAD: What's the difference between a piano, a tuna, and glue?
KID: What?
DAD: **You can tune a piano, but you can't piano a tuna.**
KID: What about the glue?
DAD: **I knew you'd get stuck there.**

What do you call a group of killer whales playing instruments? **An Orca-stra.**

Did you hear about the painter who was hospitalized? **They say it was due to too many strokes.**

Knock knock.
Who's there?
Daisy.
Daisy who?
Daisy me rollin, they hatin'.

What kind of music do mummies like?
Rap.

Why couldn't the kid see the pirate movie?
Because it was rated arrr!

What is Beethoven's favorite fruit?
Ba-na-na-naaaaaaa.

I made a playlist for hiking. It has music from Peanuts, The Cranberries, and Eminem. **I call it my Trail Mix.**

Knock knock.
Who's there?
Turnip.
Turnip who?
Turnip the volume, I love this song!

I thought my wife was joking when she said she'd leave me if I didn't stop singing "I'm a Believer"... **then I saw her face.**

What concert costs only 45 cents?
50 cent, featuring Nickelback.

What is Mozart doing right now?
Decomposing.

Me and my friends are in a band called Duvet. **We're a cover band.**

What did Michael Jackson name his denim store?
Billy Jeans!

I was in an '80s band called The Prevention. **We were better than The Cure.**

Some people say I never got over my obsession with Phil Collins. **But take a look at me now.**

Why did Mozart kill all his chickens?
Because when he asked them who the best composer was, they'd all say "Bach Bach Bach!"

So two snare drums and
a cymbal fall off a cliff...
Ba-dum-tshhh!

What is red and smells like blue paint?
Red paint!

I'm obsessed
with collecting
vinyl Beatles
albums. **I really
need "Help!"**

How many hipsters does it take to
change a lightbulb?
**Oh, it's a really obscure number.
You've probably never heard of it.**

I went to a Foo Fighters Concert once...
It was "Everlong."

BOOKS

What is the tallest building in the world?
The library—it's got the most stories!

I couldn't get a
reservation at the
library. **They were
completely booked.**

What's Harry Potter's favorite way
to get to the bottom of a hill?
Walking. J.K., rolling.

J. D. Salinger considered giving up writing
to play music in clubs. **He wanted to be DJ
Salinger.**

I was at the library and asked if they have
any books on paranoia. **The librarian
replied, "They are right behind you."**

I've just been reading a book about anti-gravity—it's impossible to put down!

I just read a book about Stockholm syndrome. **It was pretty bad at first, but I was captivated and by the end I kinda liked it.**

I just wrote a book on reverse psychology. **Do not read it!**

I bought the world's worst thesaurus yesterday. **Not only was it terrible, it was terrible.**

I'm reading a book on the history of glue. **I can't seem to put it down.**

It was easy for me to master reading braille books. **Once I got a feel for it.**

I went to a book store and asked the saleswoman where the Self Help section was. **She said if she told me it would defeat the purpose.**

A backwards poet writes inverse.

Why is Peter Pan always flying? **Because he Neverlands.**

I recently wrote a book on bricks. **Looking back, paper would have been easier.**

You know who's leaving Friday? **Robinson Crusoe.**

Today, my son asked, "Can I have a bookmark?" I burst into tears. He's 11 years old and he still doesn't know my name is Brian.

What stories do cows tell each other at bedtime? **Dairy tales.**

Whose name always rings a bell? **Quasimodo.**

A book just fell on my head. **I only have my shelf to blame.**

I accidentally swallowed a dictionary today. **It gave me thesaurus throat I've ever suffered.**

When I'm really stressed I go to the auto parts store. **Sometimes I just need a brake.**

What does a pirate pay for his corn?
A buccaneer!

I asked my friend, Nick, if he had five cents I could borrow. **But he was Nicholas.**

Can February march?
No, but April may.

I used to think I was indecisive, **but now I'm not sure.**

Yesterday a clown held a door open for me. **I thought it was a nice jester.**

What's blue and not very heavy? **Light blue.**

You know what they say about cliffhangers...

What's brown and sounds like a bell? **Dung!**

Knock knock. Who's there? Woo. Woo who? **Don't get so excited, it's just a joke.**

I just found out I'm colorblind. **The diagnosis came completely out of the red.**

What do you mean June is over? **Julying.**

Knock knock.
Who's there?
Nana.
Nana who?
Nana your business.

Why do we drive on parkways and park on driveways?

Why do dads feel the need to tell such bad jokes? **They just want to help you become a groan up.**

Imagine if alarm clocks hit you back in the morning. **It would be truly alarming.**

What do you call an old snowman? **Water.**

A quick shoutout to all of the sidewalks out there... **thanks for keeping me off the streets.**

Knock knock.
Who's there?
Hatch.
Hatch who?
Bless you!

People are making apocalypse jokes like there's no tomorrow.

Knock knock.
Who's there?
Armageddon.
Armageddon who?
Armageddon a little tired of telling knock-knock jokes.

Where do bad rainbows go? **Prism. But they only get a light sentence.**

If you're American going into the bathroom, what are you in the bathroom? **European.**

DAD: You've gotta hand it to short people.
WIFE: Why?
DAD: **Because they can't reach it.**

Poop jokes aren't my favorite kind of jokes. **But they're a solid number two.**

What question did the snowman keep asking? **"Does anyone else smell carrots?"**

I had a hand in the puppet show.

What do you
do when
balloons are
hurt?
You helium.

KID: What's up, Dad?
DAD: **The sky. The sky
is up, kiddo.**

I made a pencil
with two erasers.
It was pointless.

What does
Batman like
in his drinks?
Just ice.

A recent survey revealed six out of seven dwarves aren't happy.

Did you hear the joke about the wandering nun? **She was a Roman Catholic.**

DAD: What did you eat under there?
KID: Under where?
DAD: **YOU ATE UNDERWEAR?!**

What you seize is what you get.

People say I look better without glasses, **but I just can't see it.**

Do you know where I store all these dad jokes? **In a dadabase.**

What do you call a girl between two posts? **Annette.**

Knock knock. Who's there? **Mikey.** Mikey who? **Mikey doesn't fit in the keyhole!**

I heard that the post office was a male-dominated industry.

How do you find Will Smith in the snow? **Look for fresh prints.**

Want to hear a joke about paper?
Nevermind, it's tearable.

The magazine about ceiling fans went out of business due to low circulation.

WIFE: Can you put the trash out?
DAD: **I didn't know it was on fire!**

I have a fear of speed bumps. **I'm slowly getting over it.** I also have a fear of elevators, **but I've started taking steps to avoid it.**

Where do mermaids see movies?
The dive-in.

You can't plant any flowers if you haven't botany.

Never criticize someone until you have walked a mile in their shoes. **That way, when you criticize them, you'll be a mile away, and you'll have their shoes.**

Why didn't the toilet paper make it across the road? **It got stuck in a crack.**

I dove into the sea today. **My friend's pier pressured me into it.**

Knock knock.
Who's there?
Noise.
Noise who?
Noise to see you!

KID: What's E.T. Short for?
DAD: **It's because of his little legs.**

I'm done being a people pleaser. **If everyone's ok with that.**

Sure, I drink brake fluid. **But I can stop anytime!**

Knock knock.
Who's there?
Theodore.
Theodore who?
Theodore wasn't open so I knocked.

Where does a general keep his armies?
In his sleevies.

Knock knock.
Who's there?
Keith.
Keith who?
Keith me, my thweet printh!

I really love jokes about eyes—**the cornea the better.**

You know what really makes me smile? **My facial muscles.**

So what if I don't know what the word apocalypse means? **It's not the end of the world!**

What did the pirate say on his 80th birthday? **"Aye Matey!"**

If you think Thursdays are depressing, just wait two days longer. **It will be a sadder day.**

Knock knock.
Who's there?
Control Freak.
Con—
Okay, now you say, "Control Freak who?!"

What rhymes with boo and smells? **You!**

A magician is driving down the street... **But then he turned into a driveway.**

Knock knock.
Who's there?
Déjà.
Déjà who?
Knock knock!

I saw a sign that said, "Watch for children," and thought, "That's a really uneven trade."

A man is washing the car with his son. **The son asks, "Dad, can't you just use a sponge?"**

How do you get a baby alien to sleep? You rocket.

WIFE: We need to go to the baby doctor; I'm pregnant.
DAD: **Hmm... I think it'd be better if we went to an adult doctor.**

KID: Where's the bin?
DAD: **I haven't been anywhere!**

KID: Dad, are you alright?

DAD: No. I'm half left.

When does it rain money? **When there is change in the weather.**

This is my step ladder. **I never knew my real ladder.**

SON: Let me tell you what we're going to do today.

DAD: **I thought it was Father's Day not Son's day.**

SON: **It's also Sunday!**

What did the baby corn say to the mom corn? **Where's the popcorn?**

SON: Dad, have you seen my sunglasses?
DAD: **No, have you seen my dad glasses?**

I have a great joke about nepotism. **But I'll only tell it to my kids.**

Knock knock. Who's there? I'm a pile up. I'm a pile up who? **Don't be so hard on yourself.**

WIFE: The book said we can both bond with the baby. DAD: **I'll get the superglue.**

What do you call a dad that has fallen through the ice? **A Popsicle.**

Do you know the last thing my grandfather said to me before he kicked the bucket? **"Grandson, watch how far I can kick this bucket."**

Leather is great for sneaking around because it's made of hide.

What kind of pants do ghosts wear?
Boo jeans.

If you wear cowboy clothes,
are you ranch dressing?

Why did the belt go to prison?
He held up a pair of pants!

KID: Daddy, can you put on my shoes?
DAD: **I can try, but I don't think they'll fit!**

What's made of leather
and sounds like a sneeze?
A shoe.

How does the
moon cut his hair?
Eclipse it.

Knock knock.
Who's there?
Mustache.
Mustache who?
**Mustache you a
question, but I'll
shave it for later.**

I wouldn't buy
anything with
velcro. **It's a
total rip-off.**

I got a reversible jacket for my birthday,
I can't wait to see how it turns out.

What did the 0 say to the 8?
"Nice belt."

What do you call a lawn statue with an excellent sense of rhythmn?
A metro-gnome.

I used to hate facial hair, **but then it started to grow on me.**

What's a ninja's favorite type of shoes?
Sneakers!

The other day, my wife asked me to pass her lipstick, but I accidentally passed her a glue stick. **She still isn't talking to me.**

What did the hat say to the scarf? **"You can hang around. I'll just go on ahead."**

What did the bra say to the hat? **"You go on ahead, I'll give these two a lift."**

I told my wife she drew her eyebrows too high. **She seemed surprised.**

I got a new pair of gloves today but they were both lefts. **On one hand it's good, on the other hand it's just not right.**

I heard camoflage jackets are in this season. **But I've not seen any yet.**

How do you steal a coat? **You jacket.**

What kind of shoes does a lazy person wear? **Loafers.**

What do you call a shoe made out of a banana? **A slipper.**

Is there a hole in your shoe? **No... then how'd you get your foot in it?**

I made a belt out of watches once... **It was a waist of time.**

Somebody's taken my mood ring. I really don't how I feel about that.

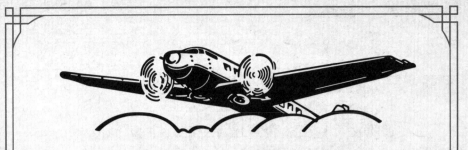

A no-fly zone prohibits zippers.

I saw my wife trip and drop a basket of clothes she'd just ironed. **I watched it all unfold.**

Why does Waldo only wear stripes? **Because he doesn't want to be spotted.**

MOM: How do I look? DAD: **With your eyes.**

If two vegans are having an argument, **is it still considered beef?**

Did you hear about the cheese that saved the world? **It was legend-dairy!**

What did Arnold Schwarzenegger say to his spaghetti? **"Pasta la vista, baby!"**

A butcher accidentally backed into his meat grinder and got a little behind in his work that day.

What did the plate say to the fork? **"Dinner is on me!"**

My wife is obsessed with her tropical fruit diet. It's enough to make a mango crazy.

What is worse than finding a worm in your apple? **Finding half a worm in your apple.**

When a dad drops a pea off of his plate: **"Oh, dear, I've pee'd on the table!"**

Knock knock.
Who's there?
Beets!
Beets who?
Beets me!

Why didn't the orange win the race? **It ran out of juice.**

What did the grape do when he got stepped on? **He let out a little wine.**

Want to hear my pizza joke?
Never mind, it's too cheesy.

I burned 2,000 calories today. I left **my dinner in the oven for too long.**

Two peanuts were walking down the street. **One was a salted.**

What do you call a cow on a trampoline? **A milk shake!**

I dreamed about drowning in an ocean made out of orange soda. **It took me a while to realize it was just a Fanta sea.**

I knew I shouldn't have ate that seafood. Because now I'm feeling a little... eel.

What did the Dorito farmer say to the other Dorito farmer? "Cool Ranch!"

What do you call cheese by itself? Provolone.

People who don't eat gluten are really going against the grain.

Knock knock.
Who's there?
Ice Cream Soda.
Ice Cream Soda who?
Ice Cream Soda whole neighborhood can hear!

Why don't seagulls fly over the bay?
Because then they'd be bay-gulls!

Today a girl said she recognized
me from vegetarian club, **but I'm
sure I've never met herbivore.**

What did the biscuit say to the
sourdough? **You're my roll model.**

Did you know the
first French fries
weren't actually
cooked in France?
**They were cooked
in Greece.**

Milk is the fastest liquid on earth.
It's pasteurized before you even see it.

My wife told me to rub the herbs on the meat for better flavor. **That's sage advice.**

What do you call a fake noodle?
An impasta.

I thought about going on an all-almond diet.
But that's just nuts.

Did you hear about the cheese factory that exploded in France?
There was nothing left but de Brie.

How does Darth Vader like his toast?
On the dark side.

Why did the tomato blush?
Because it saw the salad dressing.

What do you call corn that joins the army?
Kernel.

Why are oranges the smartest fruit?
Because they are made to concentrate.

What do you give a sick lemon?
Lemonaid.

Did you hear the one about the giant pickle?
He was kind of a big dill.

What did the late tomato say to the early tomato?
I'll ketch up.

FRUITS & VEGGIES

I'm on a whiskey diet. **I've lost three days already.**

Why don't cannibals eat clowns? **Because they taste funny.**

My friend told me that pepper is the best seasoning for a roast, **but I took it with a grain of salt.**

What biscuit does a short person like? **Shortbread.**

Have you heard the rumor going around about butter? **Never mind, I shouldn't spread it.**

I knew a guy who collected candy canes. **They were all in mint condition.**

Why did the cookie cry? **It was feeling crumby.**

I'd like to start a diet, **but I've got too much on my plate right now.**

What do you call a cow with two legs? **Lean beef.**

What do you call a cow with no legs?
Ground beef.

KID: Dad, make
me a sandwich.
DAD: Poof! You're
a sandwich.

What did the piece of
bread say to the knife?
"Butter me up."

**A cannibal is someone who
is fed up with people.**

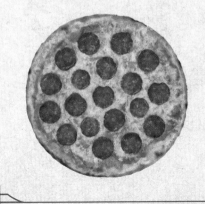

How do you fix a
broken pizza?
With tomato paste.

Why did the teddy bear say "no" to dessert? Because he was stuffed.

I cut my finger chopping cheese, but I think that I may have grater problems.

Do you know where you can get chicken broth in bulk? The stock market.

A steak pun is a rare medium well done.

What's the opposite of a croissant? A happy uncle.

What do you call cheese that doesn't belong to you? **Nacho cheese.**

I've got an addiction to water. **I think I'm an aquaholic.**

Knock knock.
Who's there?
Butter.
Butter who?
Butter be quick, I have to go to the bathroom!

What is the most attractive fruit? **A fineapple.**

What kind of bagel can fly? **A plain bagel.**

BERT: Want some ice cream?
ERNIE: Sherbert.

What's the difference between roast beef and pea soup?
Anyone can roast beef.

Knock Knock.
Who's there?
I eat mop.
I eat mop who?
Ewwwwww!

What did the cupcake say to the icing?
I'd be muffin without you.

What did the fried rice say to the shrimp?
"Don't wok away from me."

What's orange
and sounds like
a parrot?
A carrot.

Did you hear about the
carrot that died?
**There was a big turnip
at the funeral.**

What happens
when you rub two
oranges together?
Pulp friction.

What do peppers do
when they're angry?
They get jalapeño face.

DAD: Why can't you eat Wookiee meat?
SON: I don't know, why?
DAD: **Because it's too chewy.**

> **A bread pun can happen
> when you yeast expect it.**

Every time I make breakfast...
I like to propose a toast.

Knock knock.
Who's there?
Cereal.
Cereal who?
**Cereal pleasure
to meet you!**

What do you call a chicken
that's staring at lettuce?
Chicken sees a salad.

WIFE: How does the
turkey smell?
DAD: Probably
through its beak.

What did the nut say when it
was chasing the other nut?
"Imma cashew."

Yesterday, I
ate a clock. **It
was very time
consuming...
especially when
I went back
for seconds.**

I just burned this Hawaaian pizza. Guess I should have used aloha temperature.

Knock knock.
Who's there?
Cash.
Cash who?
No thanks, but I'd love some peanuts!

What happens when you eat too many SpaghettiOs?
You have a vowel movement.

Maybe hot chocolate wants to be called "beautiful chocolate" once in a while.

Don't judge a meal by the look of the first course. It's **very souperficial.**

What kind of drink can be bitter and sweet? **Reali-tea.**

I'll tell you something about German sausages: **They're the wurst.**

I relish the fact that you've mustard the strength to ketchup to me.

Murphy's Law is "anything that can go wrong will go wrong." But have you heard of Cole's Law? **It's thinly sliced cabbage.**

Have you played the updated kids' game? **I Spy With My Little Eye... Phone.**

Why did the cookie cry? **Because his mother was a wafer so long.**

A perfectionist walked into a bar... **apparently, the bar wasn't set high enough.**

Some people eat light bulbs. **They say it's a nice light snack.**

Did you hear about the new restaurant on the moon? **The menu is great, but there's just no atmosphere.**

I love waiters. **They really bring a lot to the table.**

Why does Superman get invited to dinners? **Because he is a Supperhero.**

Where do young cows eat lunch? **In the calf-ateria.**

WAITRESS: How did you find your steak? DAD: **I just looked next to the potatoes and there it was.**

Taking regular naps prevents old age, **especially if you take them when you're driving.**

What did the Zen Buddist say to the hotdog vendor? **Make me one with everything.**

A man who runs behind a car will get exhausted, but a man who runs in front of a car will get tired.

Where do hamburgers go to dance? **The meat-ball.**

HOSTESS: Do you have a preference of where you sit? DAD: **Down.**

Hear about the new restaurant called Karma? **There's no menu. You get what you deserve.**

Why did the mushroom get invited to all the parties? **Because he was a fun guy.**

The bartender says, "We don't serve time travelers in here." A time traveler walks into a bar.

A weasel walks into a bar. The bartender says, "Wow, I've never served a weasel before. What can I get for you?" "Pop," goes the weasel.

A termite walks into a bar and asks "Is the bartender here?"

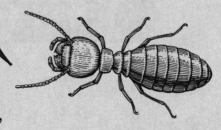

A horse walks into a bar. The bartender says "Hey." The horse says "Sure."

Two guys walked into a bar. **The third one ducked.**

A man walks into a bar with great authority, **and orders everyone around.**

I'm planning on opening a comedy club with a coffee bar. **I'm going to call it The Brew Ha Ha.**

A ghost walks into a bar and asks for a glass of vodka but the bartender says, **"Sorry, we don't serve spirits."**

A dung beetle walks to into a bar. **He asks, "Is this stool taken?"**

WAITRESS: How do you like your eggs?

DAD: **I like them just fine.**

WAITRESS: Um, how do you like them cooked?

DAD: **I like them even better that way!**

I ordered a thousand pounds of soup from the Chinese restaurant. **Won ton.**

What do you call a sketchy Italian neighborhood? **The Spaghetto.**

SERVER: Do you want a box for your leftovers?

DAD: **No. But I'll wrestle you for them!**

SERVER: Would you like your soup in a cup or bowl?

DAD: **That's a good idea, or it'll just get all over the table.**

SERVER: Soup or salad?

DAD: **Just a regular salad will be fine.**

DAD: You've got you help me, Doc. I'm addicted to Twitter.
DOCTOR: **I don't follow you.**

Hold on, I have something in my shoe. **I'm pretty sure it's a foot.**

Knock knock.
Who's there?
Ears.
Ears who?
Ears another knock-knock joke for you!

Why do vampires clean their teeth three times a day? **To prevent bat breath.**

My son saw the empty toilet paper shelves and asked if everyone would start using pull-ups. I **said, "Depends."**

Dad died because he couldn't remember his blood type. I'll never forget his last words. **Be positive.**

> When do doctors get angry?
> **When they run out of patients.**

Cosmetic surgery used to be such a touchy subject. **Now you can talk about Botox and nobody raises an eyebrow.**

DOCTOR: Do you want the good news or the bad news?
PATIENT: Good news.
DOCTOR: **We're naming a disease after you.**

> Who is the coolest doctor in the hospital?
> **The hip doctor!**

I am severely addicted to seaweed. **I must seek kelp.**

How do you make a hankie dance? **Put a little boogie in it.**

What's red and bad for your teeth? **A brick.**

I wear a stethoscope so that, in a medical emergency, **I can teach people a valuable lesson about assumptions.**

Sore throats are a pain in the neck!

What is the leading cause of dry skin? **Towels.**

Why did the tree go to the dentist? **It needed a root canal.**

What did the judge say to the dentist? **Do you swear to pull the tooth, the whole tooth, and nothing but the tooth?**

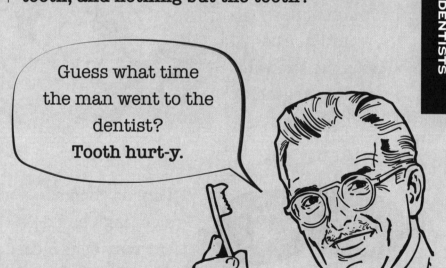

Guess what time the man went to the dentist? **Tooth hurt-y.**

What kind of award did the dentist receive? **A little plaque.**

I haven't slept for 48 hours. I really only need about eight.

I had a dream that I was a muffler last night. **I woke up exhausted!**

Why did the woman run around her bed? Because she was trying to catch up on her sleep.

I am so good at sleeping I can do it with my eyes closed!

Slept like a log last night... **woke up in the fireplace.**

Why do so many people with laser hair want to get it removed?

My sea sickness comes in waves.

Why don't ants ever get sick? Because they have anty bodies.

DOCTOR: Hello, thanks for being patient.
DAD: Hello, thanks for being doctor.

DAD: Have you heard about the movie "*Constipation?*"
WIFE: No! For real?
DAD: It hasn't come out yet.

Why is no one friends with Dracula? Because he's a pain in the neck.

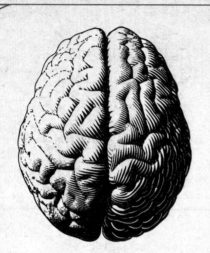

What happens when you anger a brain surgeon? **They will give you a piece of your mind.**

Mooning people is lunacy.

Where do you take someone who has been injured in a Peek-a-boo accident? **To the ICU.**

I went to the doctor today and he told me I had type A blood, **but it was a type O.**

When you have a bladder infection, **urine trouble.**

Shout out to my grandma. **That's the only way she can hear.**

Did you hear the one about the guy with the broken hearing aid? **Neither did he.**

SERVER: Are you done with the glasses? DAD: **No! I need them to see.**

What do you call ketchup with 20/20 vision? **Heinz sight.**

I've never seen the inside of my ears. But all I hear are good things!

Guess who I just bumped into on my way to get my glasses fixed? **Everybody.**

When you're homeschooling, talking to yourself is a parent-teacher conference.

I know a great joke about COVID-19, but I hope you don't get it.

What do you call a bunch of sick witches? **A covid.**

Well, on one hand there's the coronavirus... and on the other hand? **Sanitizer.**

What do you call a guy with no nose?
Nobody knows.

PERSON: Doctor, I've broken my arm in several places.
DOCTOR: **Well don't go to those places.**

How are false teeth like stars? **They come out at night.**

Why'd they call it a face mask when they could have called it a coughy filter?

Where does a boat go when it's sick?
To the dock.

How many bones are
in the human hand?
A handful of them.

I was going to get a brain transplant,
but I changed my mind.

How do hens stay fit?
They always egg-cercise.

It takes guts to be an organ donor.

A man got hit
in the head
with a can of
Coke, **but he
was alright
because it was
a soft drink.**

Technically,
all pregnant
women are...
body builders.

Did you hear about the guy whose
whole left side was cut off?
He's all right now.

Conjunctivitis.com—**now
that's a site for sore eyes.**

Why do bananas
have to put
on sunscreen
before they go to
the beach?
**Because they
might peel.**

Don't kiss anyone when you have a runny nose. **You might think it's funny, but it's snot.**

NURSE: Doctor, there's a patient that says she's invisible.
DOCTOR: **Well, tell her I can't see her right now.**

What did one eye say to the other? **"Between you and me, something smells."**

I couldn't stand to be without my legs.

I'd show you my flatter stomach... But I'm still working it out.

I was addicted to soap... **but I'm clean now.**

A massive bottle of omega-3 pills landed on me. **I'm okay, I only suffered super fish oil injuries.**

Why did the diet coach send her clients to the paint store? **She heard you could get thinner there.**

What do you get hanging from apple trees? **Sore arms.**

I had a neck brace fitted years ago. **I've never looked back since.**

I'm thinking about removing my spine. **I feel like it's only holding me back.**

One cow asked another if they were afraid of getting mad cow disease. **The other replied "Why would I? I'm a tractor."**

DAD: When this heals, will I be able to play the piano?
DOCTOR: Yes, of course.
DAD: **Great, I've always wanted to play an instrument!**

I really didn't think orthopedic shoes would help me. **But I do stand corrected.**

Did you know diarrhea is hereditary?
It runs through your jeans.

I didn't mean to gain so much weight. **It just happened by snaccident.**

What kind of music do
chiropractors like?
Hip pop.

Our maintenance guy lost his legs on
the job, **now he's just a handyman.**

Knock knock.
Who's there?
Interrupting
doctor.
Inter–
**You've got
measles.**

My back goes out more than I do.

Why did the house go to the doctor?
It was having window panes.

Dogs can't operate MRI
machines. **But catscan.**

I told my doctor I heard buzzing, **but he said it's just a bug going around.**

How many optometrists does it take to change a light bulb? **One or two? One... or two?**

I asked the surgeon if I could administer my own anesthetic, **he said, "Go ahead, knock yourself out."**

What did the green grape say to the purple grape? **"BREATHE!"**

Three years ago my doctor told me I was going deaf. **Funny, I haven't heard from him since.**

What did Romans use before
the pizza cutter was invented?
Li'l Caesars!

**Whoever invented the knock-knock
joke should get a no-bell prize.**

What's the worst thing about
ancient history class?
The teachers tend to Babylon.

Knock knock.
Who's there?
Goliath.
Goliath who?
**Goliath down,
thou looketh
tired!**

Why was it called the Dark Ages?
Because of all the knights.

Atheism is a non-prophet organization.

Where was the Declaration
of Independence signed?
At the bottom!

**To the guy on the *Titanic* who
shouted the warning "Iceberg!,"
lettuce remember him.**

Knock knock.
Who's there?
Euripides.
Euripides who?
**Euripides
jeans, you pay
for 'em.**

Why can't
you hear a
pterodactyl
going to the
bathroom?
**Because the
"p" is silent.**

What do Ivan the Terrible, Jack the
Ripper, and Attila the Hun all have
in common?
They have the same middle name.

Why was Santa's little helper feeling depressed?
Because he has low elf esteem.

What do birds give out on Halloween?
Tweets.

How do you fix a damaged jack-o-lantern?
You use a pumpkin patch.

Knock knock.
Who's there?
Ho-ho.
Ho-ho who?
You know, your Santa impression could use a little work.

Santa's helpers are subordinate clauses.

What do you call the fear of being trapped in a chimney? **CLAUStrophobia.**

The only gift I got this year was a deck of sticky playing cards. **I'm having a hard time dealing with it.**

The first thing Santa's elves have to learn in school is... **the elfabet.**

How did Anakin know what gift Obi-Wan was going to give him? **He felt his presents.**

What do you call Santa after he goes down a chimney with a fire lit? **Krisp Kringle.**

Most people don't keep to their New Year's resolutions. **Because they go in one year and out the other.**

> DAD: Good night, son.
> Happy New Year.
> SON: Happy New
> Year, Dad.
> DAD: **I'll see you...**
> SON: Don't, Dad.
> DAD: **...Next Year!**

I have this special skill that I can correctly guess what's inside a wrapped present. **It's a gift.**

Why did the turkey cross the Thanksgiving table?
To get to the other sides.

Want to hear a chimney joke?
Got tons of 'em! First one's on the house.

My father's roofing business was a great success. **But he had to stay on top of things.**

What do you get when you cross a rabbit with a water hose?
Hare spray.

There's a new type of broom out.
It's sweeping the nation.

Man, I really love my furniture.
Me and my recliner go way back.

Knock knock.
Who's there?
Aaron.
Aaron who?
Why Aaron you opening the door?

Why does a chicken coop only have two doors? **Because if it had four doors it would be a chicken sedan.**

You will never guess what Elsa did to the balloon. **She let it go.**

Knock knock.
Who's there?
Luke.
Luke who?
Luke through the the peep hole and find out.

Why are piggy banks so wise? **They're filled with common cents.**

Knock knock.
Who's there?
Dishes.
Dishes who?
Dishes a nice place you got here.

Why don't you ever shower near a Pokémon? **It'll Pikachu.**

What did one wall say to the other wall?
"I'll meet you at the corner!"

DAD: This bouncy castle is twice the price of last year.
KID: Really! Why?
DAD: **That's inflation for you.**

Don't ever try to wash dishes at the same time with someone else.
It's hard for both of you to stay in sink.

When is a door not a door?
When it's ajar.

How many South Americans does it take to change a lightbulb?
A Brazilian.

All my dad jokes are organic. **Because they're all home groan.**

Knock knock.
Who's there?
Water.
Water who?
Water those plants or they're going to die!

As I suspected, someone has been adding soil to my garden. **The plot thickens.**

I'll tell you what often gets over looked... **garden fences.**

Gardeners always know the ground rules.

The old woman who lived in a shoe wasn't the sole owner. **There were strings attached.**

Knock knock.
Who's there?
Zany.
Zany who?
Zany body home?

What does a house wear?
Address.

Knock, knock.
Who's there?
Justin.
Justin who?
Justin the neighborhood, thought I'd drop by.

I recently finished decorating our bathroom. **I didn't know what I was doing at first but I learned through tile and error.**

If dogs could build homes, what would they be great at? **Roofing.**

Knock knock.
Who's there?
Adore.
Adore who?
Adore is between us. Open up!

How does a penguin build its house? **Igloos it together.**

Have you heard the joke about the roof? **Never mind, it's over your head.**

Knock knock.
Who's there?
Dwayne.
Dwayne who?
Dwayne the bathtub already. I'm drowning!

Some mornings I wake up grumpy. **Other mornings, I let her sleep in.**

Have you heard about corduroy pillows?
They're making headlines!

Knock knock.
Who's there?
Bed.
Bed who?
**Bed you can't
guess who I am!**

How does the gingerbread
man make his bed?
He starts with a cookie sheet.

I recently swapped our bed for a
trampoline. **My wife hit the roof.**

How do you
make a water
bed more
bouncy?
**You use
spring water.**

I was just looking at my ceiling.
Not sure if it's the best ceiling in the
world, but it's definitely up there.

Knock knock.
Who's there?
Ferdie!
Ferdie who?
Ferdie last time
open this door!

Why did the kid throw the
clock out the window?
He wanted to see time fly!

Knock knock.
Who's there?
Ivor.
Ivor who?
Ivor you let me in or I'll
climb through the window.

I don't trust stairs. They're
always up to something.

LANGUAGE

What's black and white
and red all over?
The newspaper.

I bought a limited edition thesaurus
I've always wanted, but all the
pages were blank. **I have no words to
describe how angry I am.**

How many seconds
are in a year?
**Twelve. January 2nd,
February 2nd, March
2nd, April 2nd...**

Thanks for
explaining the
word "many"
to me. It
means a lot.

To be frank,
I'd have to
change my
name.

My friend said to me: "What rhymes with orange?"
I said: "No, it doesn't."

You can't run through a campground. You can only ran, because it's past tents.

Two dyslexics walk into a bra.

Why are pirates called pirates? Because they arrr!

I gave my friend ten puns, hoping that one of them would make him laugh. Sadly, no pun in ten did.

I'm glad I know sign language, **it's pretty handy.**

Yesterday I confused the words "jacuzzi" and "yakuza." **Now I'm in hot water with the Japanese mafia.**

I invented a new word! **Plagiarism.**

What is the least spoken language in the world? **Sign Language.**

What's the longest word in the dictionary? **Smiles. Because there's a mile between the two Ss.**

It's inappropriate to make a "dad joke" if you're not a dad. **It's a faux pa.**

Why do pirates not know the alphabet?
They always get stuck at "C."

I'm only familiar with
25 letters in the English
language. **I don't know why.**

The word *queue* is ironic. **It's just q with a
bunch of silent letters waiting in line.**

Knock knock.
Who's there?
Spell.
Spell who?
**Okay, fine.
W-H-O.**

Why is dark
spelled with a
k and not a c?
**Because you
can't see in the
dark.**

I read that "icy" is the easiest
word to spell. **I see why.**

When does a joke become a dad joke?
When the punchline becomes apparent.

DAD: What are you drinking, son?
SON: Soy milk.
DAD: **Hola, Milk. Soy Padre.**

What are the strongest
days on the calendar?
**Saturday and Sunday. All
the others are weekdays.**

It's hard to explain puns to kleptomaniacs,
because they take everything literally.

A number of people
have accused me of
plagiarism. **Their
word, not mine.**

I hate it when people say age is only a number. **Age is obviously a word.**

If an English teacher is convicted of a crime and doesn't complete the sentence, is that a fragment?

Knock knock.
Who's there?
To.
To who?
It's to whom.

What is the difference between ignorance and apathy?
I don't know and I don't care.

Past, present, and future walked into a bar... **It was tense.**

Quick shout out to the people asking what the opposite of "in" is.

I don't want to sound condescending. **That means I talk down to people.**

What do you call 26 letters that went for a swim? **Alphawetical.**

My wife won't talk to me because I made too many puns about birds. **Well, toucan play at that game.**

What do you call a dictionary on drugs? **High definition.**

Don't go in the bathroom for a while. **I just became public enemy number two.**

Do I enjoy making crime puns? **Guilty.**

I recently took up fencing. **The neighbors said they'll call the police unless I return the stolen goods.**

Knock knock. Who's there? Robin. Robin who? **Robin you, now hand over the cash!**

Did you hear about the two thieves who stole a calendar? **They each got six months.**

If a kid refuses to sleep during nap time... **are they resisting arrest?**

Knock knock.
Who's there?
Police.
Police who?
Police stop telling these awful knock-knock jokes!

Why did the coffee file a police report? **It got mugged.**

To the person who stole my glasses, I promise I will find you. **I have contacts.**

If prisoners could take their own mug shots, **they'd be called cellfies.**

Within minutes, the detectives knew what the murder weapon was. **It was a brief case.**

What does a CIA agent do when it's bedtime? **He goes under cover.**

The police arrested the world champion tongue-twister. **I bet he'll be getting a tough sentence.**

Knock knock.
Who's there?
FBI.
FB...
We're asking the questions here!

I just saw a burglar breaking down his own door. I asked "What are you doing?" **"Working from home," he said.**

Knock knock.
Who's there?
Dishes!
Dishes who?
Dishes the Police! Come out with your hands up.

Some people think prison is one word. **But to inmates it's a whole sentence.**

LOVE & ROMANCE

What do you call a sorcerer who likes to give hickeys? **A necromancer.**

I met my wife on a dating app and, I don't know, **we just clicked.**

Who did the sorcerer marry? **His ghoul-friend.**

Last night me and my wife watched three movies back to back. **Luckily I was the one facing the TV.**

My wife refuses to go to a nude beach with me. **I think she's just being clothes-minded.**

Knock knock.
Who's there?
Olive.
Olive who?
Olive you with all my heart!

I left my first wife because she couldn't stop counting. **I do wonder what she's up to now?**

Why don't some couples go to the gym? **Because some relationships don't work out.**

What did celery say when he broke up with his girlfriend? **"She wasn't right for me, so I really don't carrot all."**

A bartender broke up with her boyfriend, **but he kept asking her for another shot.**

Why can't eggs have love? **They will break up too soon.**

My wife and I were happy for 20 years. **Then we met.**

Where do rabbits go after they get married? **On a bunny-moon.**

A man walked in to a bar with some asphalt on his arm. **He said "Two beers please. One for me and one for the road."**

Why shouldn't you marry a tennis player? **Because love means nothing to them.**

My wife said, "You weren't even listening, were you?" **And I thought, "That's a pretty weird way to start a conversation."**

Why did the melons plan a big wedding? **Because they cantaloupe!**

My wife told me to stop impersonating a flamingo. **I had to put my foot down.**

My wife is really mad at the fact that I have no sense of direction. **So I packed up my stuff and right.**

What do you call a hippie's wife? **Mississippi.**

Did I tell you the time I fell in love during a backflip? **I was heels over head.**

For Valentine's day, I decided to get my wife some beads for an abacus. **It's the little things that count.**

How did the telephone propose to its girlfriend? **He gave her a ring.**

A persistent banker wouldn't stop hitting on me, so I asked him to leave me a loan.

What do bees do after they are married?
They go on a honeymoon.

My wife says I only have a couple of faults. I don't listen to her and... something else.

Our wedding was so beautiful, even the cake was in tiers.

My wife's mad at me because she said I never buy her flowers. **I honestly didn't even know she sold flowers.**

Why did the pasta marry the cheese? **Because they wanted to join in holy macaroni.**

An invisible man married an invisible woman. **Their kids were nothing to look at.**

Did you hear about the bunsen burner who worked with the beaker?
He had a very esteemed colleague.

Decimals do always have a point.

Never ask for advice from electrons. **They are always negative.**

Why do young girls hang out in odd numbered groups?
Because they can't even.

Never discuss infinity with a mathematician. **They can go on about it forever.**

SON: Dad, I'm cold.
DAD: **Go stand in the corner; I hear it's 90 degrees.**

Never trust someone with graph paper... **they're always plotting something.**

Why do mathematicians hate the US? **Because it's indivisible.**

Americans can't switch from pounds to kilograms overnight. **That would cause mass confusion.**

Geology rocks, but geography is where it's at!

What is bread's favorite number? Leaven.

R.I.P. boiled water. **You will be mist.**

Why can't your nose be 12 inches long? **Because then it'd be a foot!**

Why doesn't the sun go to college?
Because it has a million degrees.

Astronomers got tired watching the moon go around the earth for 24 hours. **They decided to call it a day.**

How do you organize a space party?
You planet.

The rotation of earth really makes my day.

What's it called when you have too many aliens?
Extraterrestrials.

What planet is like a circus?
Saturn, it has three rings.

What happens to nitrogen when the sun comes up? It becomes daytrogen.

A cowboy had 297 cows. **When he rounded them up, he found he had 300.**

I've been trying to come up with a dad joke about momentum... **but I just can't seem to get it going.**

What time is it? **I don't know... it keeps changing.**

Don't trust atoms. **They make up everything.**

There's a fine line between the numerator and the denominator.

Why didn't the number 4 get into the nightclub? Because he is 2 square.

Did you know that protons have mass?
I didn't even know they were Catholic.

Knock knock.
Who's there?
Dozen.
Dozen who?
**Dozen anybody want
to let me in?!**

I tried to write a
chemistry joke,
**but could never
get a reaction.**

Why was Pavlov's beard so soft?
Because he conditioned it.

**I, for one, like
Roman numerals.**

Which is the
fastest growing
city in the world?
Dublin'.

Without geometry, life is pointless.

GEOMETRY

The biggest knight
at King Arthur's
round table was
Sir Cumference.
He acquired his size
from eating too much pi.

Remember, the best angle
to approach a problem
from is the "try" angle.

Parallel lines have so much in common.
It's a shame they'll never meet.

I think circles
are pointless.

Why is the obtuse triangle
always so frustrated?
Because it is never right.

I've been attacked by 1, 3, 5, 7, and 9.
The odds were against me.

I'll do algebra,
I'll do trig. I'll
even do statistics.
**But graphing
is where I draw
the line!**

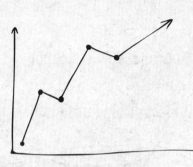

I fear for the calendar.
Its days are numbered.

They're making a
movie about clocks.
It's about time.

Why was 10
scared of seven?
**Because seven
ate nine.**

How does a scientist freshen their breath?
With experi-mints!

Did you hear about the mathematician who is afraid of negative numbers?
They'd stop at nothing to avoid them.

5/4 of people admit that they're bad with fractions.

What's the best way to count cows?
With a cowculator.

TEACHER: Why are you doing your multiplication on the floor?
STUDENT: **You told me not to use tables.**

When chemists die, we barium.

What is the internal temperature of a Tauntaun?
Luke warm.

That new burger joint was destined to go down in flames. It was called Hindenburgers.

What do you call a detective electrician? **Sherlock Ohms.**

Do you know it was a Frenchman who invented sandals? **His name was Phillipe Phillop.**

I recently received my PhD in palindromes. **I now go by Dr. Awkward.**

What do you call two guys tied up and stuck in a window? **Kurt and Rod.**

A buddy of mine named his dog "5 Miles" so he could tell people he walked 5 miles. **But today he ran over 5 Miles.**

What do you call a woman who sets fire to all her bills ? **Bernadette.**

The worst pub I've ever been in was called The Fiddle. **It was a vile inn.**

My son Luke loves that we named our children after *Star Wars* characters. **Our daughter Chewbacca, not so much.**

What was the full name of Eddie Murphy's character in *Shrek?* **Donkey Ho-tay.**

My friend Jay recently had twin girls and wanted to name them after him. **So I suggested Kaye and Elle.**

I wanted to name my son Lance, but my wife said it was too uncommon. **I told her that in medieval days, people were named Lance a lot.**

What do you call a guy lying on your doorstep? **Matt.**

My favorite teacher at school was Mrs. Turtle. **Strange name but she tortoise well.**

What do you call a magician who has lost their magic? **Ian.**

My wife threatened to divorce me when I said I was going to give our daughter a silly name. **So I called her Bluff.**

What does a lawyer name his daughter? **Sue.**

I have an Irish friend with a great personality who always bounces off the walls. **His name is Rick O'Shea.**

Did you hear about the watchmaker who is half Spanish and half Irish? **His name is Juan O'Clock.**

I just found out that Bill Nye is just a stage name. **His real name is William New Year's Eve.**

MAN: You want me to write a kids song about a dog with a funny "name-o"?
DAD: **Bingo.**

Did you hear David Hasslehoff has changed his name to David Hoff? **He just couldn't deal with the Hassle anymore.**

Did you hear about the incredibly average philosopher?
His name was Mediocrates.

My friend Victor recently changed his last name to "E" but no-one knows why... **He's become a Mr. E.**

What do you call a friend who stands in a hole?
Phil.

I don't really know who Pavlov is. But it rings a bell.

What's the most ironic name for a vegan?
Hunter.

What do you call a man with a rubber toe? **Roberto.**

I have a pure bread dog. **His name is fidough.**

What did the the drummer call his twin daughters? **Anna one, Anna two!**

There was a street named Chuck Norris. **But they had to change it because no one crosses Chuck Norris and lives.**

What do you call a man who can't stand? **Neil.**

If I have twin daughters, I'll name one Kate. **And I'll name the other Duplikate.**

What do you call a boy who stopped digging holes? **Douglas.**

Did you hear about the campsite that got visited by Bigfoot?
It got in tents.

If you walk into a forest and cut down a tree, but the tree doesn't understand why, **it's stumped.**

Do you want a brief explanation of what an acorn is?
In a nutshell, it's an oak tree.

Don't tell secrets in corn fields.
Too many ears around.

How was the snow globe feeling after the storm?
A little shaken.

What's brown and sticky?
A stick.

Why do trees seem suspicious
on sunny days?
Dunno, they're just a bit shady.

This morning I was wondering where the
sun was, **but then it dawned on me.**

Knock knock.
Who's there?
Leaf.
Leaf who?
Leaf me alone!

What kind of
tree fits in your
hand?
A palm tree!

**After winter,
the trees
are relieved.**

What did the big flower
say to the little flower?
"Hi, bud!"

How do
mountains
see?
They peak.

What did the
ocean say to
the shore?
**Nothing; it
just waved.**

What lies at the
bottom of the ocean
and twitches?
A nervous wreck.

Why are there
fish at the bottom
of the sea?
**Because they
dropped out
of school.**

Why is the ocean
always blue?
**Because the shore
never waves back.**

What did the ocean say to the beach?
"Thanks for all the sediment."

Some moss took a lichen to a tree.

What did the beaver say to the tree?
"It's been nice gnawing you!"

Knock knock.
Who's there?
Teresa.
Teresa who?
Teresa are green!

How many apples grow on a tree?
All of them.

MOM: Is the moon waxing or waning?
DAD: **Waning? It isn't even cwoudy.**

What did the shy pebble wish for?
That she was a little boulder.

A plateau is a high form of flattery.

What kind of shorts do clouds wear?
Thunderwear.

Mountains aren't just funny.
They're hill areas.

Why do
trees have
so many
friends?
**They
branch out.**

Before Mount
Rushmore was
carved, its natural
beauty was...
Unpresidented.

What did daddy
spider say to
baby spider?
**"You spend too
much time on
the web."**

What did the sushi say to the bee?
"Wasabee!"

What do you do when your bunny gets wet?
You get your hare dryer.

You can never lose a homing pigeon. **Because if it doesn't come back it's just a regular pigeon.**

Not sure when my little pet snake will arrive. **But he won't be long.**

What do you call a rabbit with fleas?
Bugs bunny.

My dog has no nose. Guess how he smells?
Awful.

I feel bad. Every time I ask my dog how his day was, **he always says "ruff."**

Why was the big cat disqualified from the race? **Because it was a cheetah.**

My cat was just sick on the carpet. **I don't think it's feline well.**

My dog used to chase people on a bike a lot. **It got so bad I had to take his bike away.**

Why did the cowboy have a weiner dog? **Somebody told him to get a long little doggy.**

What do you call a group of disorganized cats? **A cat-astrophe.**

Where do cats write notes?
Scratch paper!

I adopted my dog from a blacksmith. **As soon as we got home he made a bolt for the door.**

What do you call a dog that can do magic tricks? **A labracadabrador.**

What do you get when you cross a centipede and a parrot? **A walkie-talkie.**

It was raining cats and dogs the other day. I almost stepped in a poodle.

Put the cat out. **I didn't realize it was on fire!**

DAD: A three-legged dog walks into a bar. Guess what he said to the bartender?
SON: Stop, Dad.
DAD: **"I'm lookin' for the man who shot my paw."**

What did the dog say to the two trees?
Bark bark.

My password has been hacked again. **That's the fourth time I've had to rename our cat.**

What do you call a donkey that only has three legs? **A wonkey!**

What do you call a pile of cats? **A Meowtain.**

What's the difference between a dog and a marine biologist? **One wags a tail and the other tags a whale.**

What do you call the ghost of a chicken?
A poultry-geist.

Knock knock.
Who's there?
Witches.
Witches who?
Witches the way to Hogwarts.

What is the hardest part about sky diving?
The ground.

If you think swimming with dolphins is expensive, **you should try swimming with sharks—it cost me an arm and a leg!**

Did you hear about the monster bicycle that was biting people's arms off?
It was a vicious cycle.

People saying "Boo!" to their friends has risen by 85% in the last year...
That's a frightening statistic.

A woman is on trial for beating her husband to death with his guitar collection. The judge asks, "First offender?" **She says, "No, first a Gibson! Then a Fender!"**

Why don't skeletons ever go trick or treating? **Because they have no-body to go with.**

How does a French skeleton say hello? **Bone-jour.**

DAD: All of the people who live around here aren't allowed to be buried in that cemetery.
SON: Really? Why?
DAD: **Because they're not dead yet.**

Organ donors really put their heart into it.

Why are skeletons so calm? **Because nothing gets under their skin.**

Models of dragons are not to scale.

You know that cemetery up the road? People are dying to get in there.

How do you know when you're going to drown in milk? **When it's past your eyes!**

Knock knock.
Who's there?
Boo.
Boo who?
Aw, don't cry!

Why are ghosts bad liars? **Because you can see right through them!**

A skeleton walked into a bar... **he said, "Give me a beer and a mop."**

What do snails become when they die? **Escarghosts.**

The tale of the haunted refrigerator was chilling.

What is a vampire's favorite fruit?
A blood orange.

A man was caught stealing in a supermarket today while balanced on the shoulders of a couple of vampires. **He was charged with shoplifting on two counts.**

If you ever come across a vampire snowman, **watch out for frostbite.**

How can you tell a vampire has a cold?
They start coffin.

Why did Dracula lie in the wrong coffin?
He made a grave mistake.

Why are graveyards so noisy?
Because of all the coffin.

A fortune teller told me in 12 years time,
I'd suffer terrible heartbreak.
So to cheer myself up, I bought a puppy.

Why didn't the skeleton cross the road?
Because he had no guts.

What do
you call a
careful wolf?
Aware wolf.

Why do ghosts
speak Latin?
Because it's a
dead language.

A man tried to sell
me a coffin today...
I told him that was
the last thing I'd
need.

Why are mummies scared of vacation?
They're afraid to unwind.

Why don't skeletons ride roller coasters?
They don't have the stomach for it.

Bees can still sting you when they're dead. **They're zombees.**

Do you think glass coffins will be a success? **Remains to be seen.**

Why didn't the skeleton play golf?
His heart wasn't in it.

After eating the ship, the sea monster said, **I can't believe I ate the hull thing.**

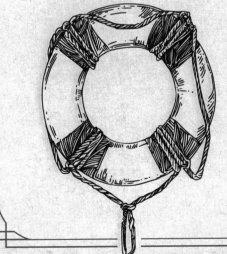

Why couldn't the lifeguard save the hippie?
He was too far out, man.

What do scholars snack on when they're hungry?
Academia nuts.

What did the buffalo say to his little boy when he dropped him off at school?
Bison.

What did the calculator say to the student?
You can count on me.

To the guy who invented zero...
thanks for nothing.

What do you call a duck that gets all As?
A wise quacker.

What's the worst part about being a cross-eyed teacher? **They can't control their pupils.**

Where did you learn to make ice cream? **Sundae school.**

What is a witch's favorite subject in school? **Spelling!**

Why do magicians do so well in school? **They're good at trick questions.**

I got an A on my origami assignment when I turned my paper into my teacher.

An apple a day keeps the bullies away.
If you throw it hard enough.

Why did the
kid cross the
playground?
**To get to the
other slide.**

Why does the
teacher wear
sunglasses to
school? **She has
bright students.**

Did you hear
about the
kidnapping
at school?
**It's okay. He
woke up.**

Whiteboards...
are remarkable!

SHOPPING

Whenever the grocery cashier asks me if I would like the milk in a bag, **I say, "No, just leave it in the carton!"**

So a duck walks into a pharmacy and says, "Give me some chapstick... **and put it on my bill."**

Dad walks into a lumberyard to buy some two-by-fours for a deck.
CLERK: How long do you need them?
DAD: **For a pretty long time.**

I bought shoes from a drug dealer once. **I don't know what he laced them with, but I was tripping all day.**

I really want to buy one of those supermarket checkout dividers, **but the cashier keeps putting it back.**

CASHIER: $19.89.
DAD: **Ah... That was a terrific year.**

Where did Captain Hook get his hook? **From a second-hand store.**

Don't buy flowers at a monastery. **Because only you can prevent florist friars.**

The great thing about stationery shops is they're always in the same place.

I heard there was a new store called Moderation. **They have everything there.**

I ordered a chicken and an egg from Amazon. **I'll let you know which comes first.**

What kind of bird likes to go shopping? **A Pottery Barn Owl.**

What do you call two monkeys that share an Amazon account? **Prime mates.**

Did you hear the news? FedEx and UPS are merging. **They're going to go by the name Fed-Up from now on.**

WAITER: Here's your check. Can I get you anything else?

DAD: **How about someone else to pay for it.**

Chances are if you've seen one shopping center, **you've seen a mall.**

I went to the store to pick up eight cans of Sprite... **When I got home, I realized I'd only picked seven up.**

I saw an ad in a shop window: "Television for sale, $1, volume stuck on full." **I thought, "I can't turn that down."**

Ebay is so useless. **I tried to look up lighters and all they had was 12,579 matches.**

DAD: Did you hear about the shortages at the stores?

FRIEND: The TP?

DAD: **Yeah. They're all wiped out.**

SPORTS & GAMES

I don't play soccer because I want to play professionally. **I'm just doing it for kicks.**

Camping is intense.

Did you hear about the runner who was criticized? **She just took it in stride.**

I had a pair of racing snails. I removed their shells to make them more aerodynamic, **but they became sluggish.**

Did you know you should always take an extra pair of pants golfing? **Just in case you get a hole in one.**

At the boxing match a guy got into the popcorn line and the line for hot dogs, **but he wanted to stay out of the punchline.**

I haven't been to the gym for such a long time, **I've gone back to calling it James.**

If at first you don't succeed, **sky diving is not for you!**

What do you call a crowd of chess players bragging about their wins in a hotel lobby? **Chess nuts boasting in an open foyer.**

Why are basketball players messy eaters? **Because they are always dribbling.**

Someone broke into my house last night and stole my limbo trophy. **How low can you go?**

What is a tornado's favorite game to play? **Twister!**

Why does it take longer to get from 1st to 2nd base, than it does to get from 2nd to 3rd base? **Because there's a shortstop in between!**

Is the pool safe for diving?
It deep ends.

I was wondering why the frisbee was getting bigger, **then it hit me.**

Why is Cinderella so bad at soccer?
She always runs away from the ball.

Don't interrupt someone working intently on a puzzle. Chances are, you'll hear some crosswords.

Sometimes I tuck my knees into my chest and lean forward. **That's just how I roll.**

Why do scuba divers fall backwards into the water?
Because if they fell forwards they'd still be in the boat.

Why is it so windy inside an arena?
All those fans.

Why did the football coach go to the bank?
To get his quarterback.

I was so proud when I finished the jigsaw in six months, when on the side of the box it said three to four years.

What do you call a boomerang that doesn't come back?
A stick.

What was the pumpkin's favorite sport?
Squash.

Today a man knocked on my door and asked for a small donation towards the local swimming pool. **I gave him a glass of water.**

Bad at golf?
Join the club.

What did the mountain climber name his son?
Cliff.

I used to be afraid of the hurdles, **but I got over it.**

Did you hear about the runner who was criticized? **She just took it in stride.**

What do you call a nervous javelin thrower? **Shakespeare.**

How did the barber win the race? **He took a short cut.**

What do sprinters eat before a race? **Nothing—they fast.**

I believe my wife put glue on my firearms. Of course, she denies it but I'm sticking to my guns.

Why does the man want to buy nine rackets? 'Cause tennis too many.

Why isn't suntanning an Olympic sport? Because the best you can ever get is bronze.

Why is an octopus such a great football player? Because they get ten tackles every game.

You don't need a parachute to go skydiving, but you need a parachute to go skydiving twice.

Have you ever tried blindfolded archery? You don't know what you're missing.

TECHNOLOGY

Why are hungry clocks unreliable?
They always go back four seconds.

A guy told me today he did not know what cloning is. I told him, "That makes two of us."

Toasters were the first form of pop-up notifications.

Why did Sweden start painting barcodes on the sides of their battleships? **So they could Scandinavian.**

My sister bet me $50 that I couldn't build a car out of spaghetti. **You should have seen the look on her face as I drove pasta.**

Breaking news! Energizer Bunny arrested—**charged with battery.**

Why can't you use "Beef stew" as a password?
Because it's not stroganoff.

The first time I got a universal remote control I thought to myself, **"This changes everything."**

What did the digital clock say to the grandfather clock?
"Look, no hands!"

I saw a documentary on TV last night about how they put ships together. **It was riveting.**

What do slow computers and air conditioners have in common? **They both become useless when you open windows.**

What does a baby computer call his father? **Data!**

What do you call a computer that sings? **A-Dell.**

My computer is so slow it hertz.

Why was the computer late for work? **He had a slow hard drive.**

How do the trees get on the internet?
They log on.

Two fish are in a tank, one turns to the other and says, **"How do you drive this thing?"**

What's the best time of day?
Six-thirty, hands down!

I gave all my dead batteries away today, **free of charge.**

What do prisoners use to call each other?
Cell phones.

SON: Dad, can I watch the TV?
DAD: **Sure, just don't turn it on.**

What's the best thing about
elevator jokes?
They work on so many levels.

I asked a Frenchman
if he played video
games. **He said "Wii."**

Have you heard of the band 1023MB?
They haven't got a gig yet.

I needed a password
eight characters long,
**so I picked Snow White
and the Seven Dwarfs.**

Hear about the
claustrophobic
astronaut?
**He just needed a
little space.**

Two wrongs don't make a right...
but two Wrights did make an airplane.

DAD: Y'know what was a truly groundbreaking innovation?
KID: Ugh, dad. **Please don't say a shovel.**
DAD: *Finger guns*

Egyptians claimed to invent the guitar, **but they were such lyres.**

What was a more important invention than the first telephone?
The second one.

The Swiss must've been pretty confident in their chances of victory if they included a corkscrew in their army knife.

The invention of the wheel was what got things rolling.

My first time using an elevator was an uplifting experience. The second time let me down.

Knock knock.
Who's there?
CD.
CD who?
CD guy on your doorstep?

The reason it's so hard to wake up in the morning is Newton's First Law. **A body at rest wants to stay at rest.**

I decided to sell my vacuum cleaner. **All it was doing was collecting dust.**

Why was the robot angry? **Because someone kept pushing his buttons!**

How much does an influencer weigh? **An Instagram.**

Two satellites decided to get married. **The wedding wasn't much, but the reception was incredible.**

What do you do on a remote island? **Try and find the TV island it belongs to.**

A police officer caught two kids playing with a car battery and a firework. **He charged one and let the other one off.**

My vacuum doesn't work. **It blows.**

What has three letters and starts with gas? **A Car.**

To the person that stole my Microsoft Office, I will find you. **On that, you have my Word.**

What do you call a droid that takes the long way around? **R2 detour.**

Knock knock.
Who's there?
Zoom.
Zoom who?
Zoom did you expect!

What do you call a bee that lives in America? **A USB.**

I've deleted the phone numbers of all the Germans I know from my mobile phone. **Now it's Hans-free.**

My friend has invented an invisible airplane. **I really can't see it taking off.**

I was going to tell you a time-traveling joke, but you didn't like it.

Guess what Forrest Gump's password is? **It's 1forrest1.**

Why did Microsoft PowerPoint cross the road? **To get to the other slide.**

I tried taking some high-resolution photos of local farmland, **but they all turned out a bit grainy.**

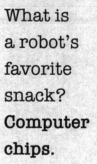

What is a robot's favorite snack? **Computer chips.**

TECH SUPPORT: How can I help you?
DAD: **I need to uninstall and reinstall something... 2020. It has a nasty virus.** [Click, dial tone]

I thought I saw a spider on my laptop, **but my friend said it was just a bug.**

What do you call crystal clear urine? **1080pee.**

What washes up on tiny beaches? **Microwaves.**

My son kept chewing on electrical cords, **so I had to ground him. He's** doing better currently and conducting himself properly.

Did you hear that David lost his ID?
Now we just have to call him Dav.

DAD: Knock Knock.
KID: Who's there?
DAD: Europe
KID: Europe Who?
DAD: **How dare you call me that!**

I once tripped when I was in Paris.
Eiffel over.

What's the advantage of living in Switzerland?
Well, the flag is a big plus.

What did the red light say to the green light?
Don't look at me, I'm changing!

How do locomotives know where they're going?
Lots of training.

Knock knock.
Who's there?
Alpaca.
Alpaca who?
Alpaca the trunk, you pack the suitcase.

A man sued an airline company after it lost his luggage. **Sadly, he lost his case.**

A red and a blue ship have just collided in the Caribbean. **Apparently the survivors are marooned.**

Why did the girl smear peanut butter on the road?
To go with the traffic jam.

I was thinking about moving to Moscow, **but I don't like to Russian to things.**

Why can't bicycles stand up on their own?
They're two tired.

Knock knock.
Who's there?
Hawaii.
Hawaii who?
**I'm fine,
Hawaii you?**

What sound
does a witches
car make?
Broom, Broom.

They don't allow
loud laughing
in Hawaii. **Just
a low ha.**

Why do birds fly south for the winter?
Because it's too far to walk.

Finland has just closed their borders.
No-one's going to be crossing the finish line.

Reversing the car
Ah, this takes me back!

What happens to a frog's car when it breaks down? **It gets toad.**

Knock knock.
Who's there?
Cargo.
Cargo who?
No, car go "beep beep"!

I saw an ad for a Delorean with low miles. **It said it's only been driven from time to time.**

What do you do when you see a space man? **Park your car, man.**

I couldn't figure out how the seat belt worked. **Then it just clicked.**

What's the most detail-oriented ocean?
The Pacific.

I don't get why people buy into the flat earth theory. **I mean, the arguments for it aren't even well rounded.**

I tried to catch the fog yesterday. **Entirely mist.**

Why should you never trust a train? **They have loco motives.**

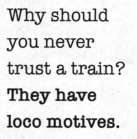

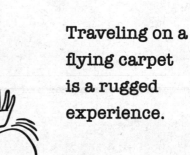

Traveling on a flying carpet is a rugged experience.

What jam can't you eat? **Traffic jam.**

I quit working at the concrete plant. **My job kept getting harder and harder.**

I used to work as a soft drink can crusher. **It was soda pressing.**

Why did the invisible man turn down the job offer?
He couldn't see himself doing it!

My wife asked me to do some odd jobs. **She gave me a list of 10, so I only did numbers 1, 3, 5, 7, and 9.**

BOSS: It's highly suspicious that you are only sick on weekdays.
DAD: **It must be my weekend immune system.**

I used to work in a shoe-recycling shop. **It was sole crushing.**

Why did the worker get fired from the orange juice factory? **Lack of concentration.**

I broke my finger at work today. **On the other hand, I'm completely fine.**

There's not really any training for garbagemen. **They just pick things up as they go.**

Did you hear about the submarine industry? **It really took a dive.**

A beekeeper was indicted after he confessed to years of stealing at work. **They charged him with emBEEzlement.**

Why did the scarecrow win an award? **Because he was outstanding in his field.**

Every machine in the coin factory broke down all of a sudden without explanation. **It just doesn't make any cents.**

It's difficult to say what my wife does— **she sells sea shells by the sea shore.**

Why did the miner get fired from his job?
He took it for granite.

I never wanted to believe that my Dad was stealing from his job as a road worker. **But when I got home, all the signs were there.**

I applied to be a doorman but didn't get the job due to lack of experience. **That surprised me, I thought it was an entry-level position.**

Want to hear a joke about construction? Nah, I'm still **working on it.**

I used to work at a stationery store. **But, I didn't feel like I was going anywhere.** So, I got a job at a travel agency. **Now, I know I'll be going places.**

I went on a date last night with a woman from the zoo. It was great. **She's a keeper.**

I started a new business making yachts in my attic this year. **The sails are going through the roof.**

Did you hear about the guy who invented Lifesavers? **They say he made a mint.**

I wish I could clean mirrors for a living. **It's just something I can see myself doing.**

Why did the burglar hang his mugshot on the wall?
To prove that he was framed!

You can't trust a ladder.
It will always let you down.

It doesn't matter how much you push the envelope. **It will still be stationary.**

If anyone gets an email from me about canned meat, don't open it—**it's spam.**

Why was the broom late for the meeting? **He overswept.**

My boss told me to have a good day. **So I went home.**

BOSS: How good are you at PowerPoint?
DAD: **I Excel at it.**
BOSS: Was that a Microsoft Office pun?
DAD: **Word.**
BOSS: You're fired.

I hate perforated lines. **They're tearable.**

Some people say that comedians who tell too many light bulb jokes soon burn out, but they don't know watt they are talking about. They're not that bright.

I was fired from the keyboard factory yesterday. I wasn't putting in enough shifts.

Why did the man put his money in the freezer? He wanted cold, hard cash!

I'm tired of following my dreams. I'm just going to ask them where they are going and meet up with them later.

Knock knock.
Who's there?
Amanda.
Amanda who?
Amanda fix your sink!

My boss told me to put together two pieces of wood. I totally nailed it!

In my career as a lumberjack I cut down exactly 52,487 trees. **I know because I kept a log.**

I used to be a banker, **but I lost interest.**

I knew I shouldn't steal a mixer from work, **but it was a whisk I was willing to take.**

Did you hear about the bread factory burning down? **They say the business is toast.**

If you want a job in the moisturizer industry, **the best advice I can give is to apply daily.**

My son is studying to be a surgeon. **I just hope he makes the cut.**

People are usually shocked when they find out I'm a terrible electrician.

I just got fired from a garden nursery. **Apparently, I took too many leaves.**

Where are adequate things built? **In the satisfactory.**

I finally got my dream job where they make guillotines. **I'll beheading there shortly.**

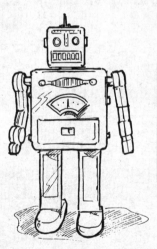

What would the Terminator be called in his retirement? **The Exterminator.**

I used to have a job at a calendar factory, **but I was fired because I took a couple of days off.**

People at work are too judgmental. **I can tell just by looking at them.**

DAD: Sorry I'm late. I was having computer trouble.
BOSS: Hard drive?
DAD: **No, the commute was fine. It's my laptop.**

How do lawyers say goodbye? **"We'll be suing ya!"**

I used to have an origami business, **but it folded.**

Don't trust acupuncturists. **They're backstabbers.**

I know a ton of jokes about retired people, **but none of them really work.**

Archeologists' careers are in ruins.

My grandmother used to say, "The way to a man's heart is through his stomach." **Lovely lady, horrific surgeon.**

INTERVIEWER: Can you perform under pressure? DAD: **I'm not sure about that, but I can have a good crack at "Bohemian Rhapsody."**

Why did the fireman wear red, white, and blue suspenders? **To hold his pants up.**

I lost my job at the bank on my first day. **A woman asked me to check her balance, so I pushed her over.**

My boss told me that he was going to fire the person with the worst posture. **I have a hunch it might be me.**